Circles of Belonging

Rick Richardson

InterVarsity Press
P.O. Box 1400, Downers Grove, IL 60515-1426
World Wide Web: www.ivpress.com
E-mail: mail@ivpress.com

*InterVarsity Press® is the book-publishing division of InterVarsity Christian
Fellowship/USA®, a student movement active on campus at hundreds of
universities, colleges and schools of nursing in the United States of America, and
a member movement of the International Fellowship of Evangelical Students.
For information about local and regional activities, write Public Relations
Dept., InterVarsity Christian Fellowship/USA, 6400 Schroeder Rd., P.O. Box
7895, Madison, WI 53707-7895.*

ISBN 0-87784-053-9

Printed in the United States of America ∞

15	14	13	12	11	10	9	8	7	6	5	4	3	2
11	10	09	08	07	06	05	04	03	02	01			

Who am I?

Where do I belong?

Where will I find love?

Have you ever asked yourself these questions?

I know I have. Often.

In my last year in high school I was consumed by those questions. It started on a bus ride, a ski trip to northern Pennsylvania with my high-school ski club. Several rows from the back seat of the bus, where I liked to hang out, I saw a cascade of blond hair falling over the back of a seat. I thought, *That looks intriguing.* So I decided to make my way forward to join John, my friend who liked to hang out in the front seat of the bus.

I neglected to think up anything to say to John. So I felt a little foolish as our conversation stalled. But I quickly forgot my embarrassment as I went back to my seat. Yes! That cascade of blond hair was definitely intriguing! *Maybe I'll run into her out on the slopes,* I hoped.

After my third time down, as I stood at the bottom of the run, I looked up the slope to see a person hurtling in my general direction, blond hair streaming behind. She flashed by me and collided with a nearby woman. I hurried over. Concerned about both victims of the wipeout, I asked Blond Hair if she was OK. "Yes, I'm fine," she responded. I helped her up.

"My name is Rick."

"My name is Karen."

And we were on our way! The next time down we skied together. Halfway down, I waited. There she came again, hurtling down the slope, blond hair streaming. Again she flashed by me, and this time she collided with a young man.

Concerned about both of the tumblers, once again I skied over to Karen, helped her up, asked her if she was OK. "Yes, I'm fine!" And off we went again.

At the bottom of the hill I waited for her. This time when she flew past me there was no one to "catch" her. I winced as she came to a full and ungraceful stop against the big picture window of the lodge, those inside looking out at her with alarm and wonder in their eyes.

"Karen, I'm noticing a pattern. You seem to get along well until it comes to the stopping part, and then things seem to get fairly dramat-ic."

"Yeah, nobody ever taught me how to stop these things!" she responded, looking down at her skis.

"I'd be glad to help." So I taught her to shush and snowplow and stop—to the great delight of everyone who had had the opportunity of be-coming acquainted with Karen on the slopes!

At the end of the evening I asked Karen out. I had to ask several times over the next several evenings, because she had just broken up with someone, but she finally agreed. Little did I know that sailing along fine followed by crash-and-burn endings on the slopes was a pattern that would also come to characterize our rela-tionship. Had I known, I would have helped the other hapless tumblers and let Karen fend for herself.

We just never seemed to be able to communicate well. And I will never forget the prom night from hell. We did fine until midnight. But somehow, when it came to the kissing part, she got upset about something I'd done, blew me off and got another ride home.

Two weeks later the inevitable happened. She told me she didn't want to date anymore. Then she let me know she had never really been attracted to me and that it had been a mistake to ever go out. This was after six months of fairly intense dating.

Flight from Rejection

Have you ever felt rejection like that? It stays in the pit of your stomach, sometimes for months. That experience brought out all my loneliness, all my longing for acceptance and belonging, all my need to feel good about who I was and how I looked.

Many of us have those needs and longings. We want to know we're accepted for who we are, that someone thinks we're special and attractive. We want to feel at home with ourselves and at least a few other people.

Some of us grew up in families that fell apart. Some of us grew up in families that never really grew together. In my family it was very hard to express affection, to ask for what I needed, to trust that I was known and loved for who I was. Maybe it was that way in your family too.

After the breakup with Karen, I went into a shell and built a wall around myself. But I still needed to feel loved, to belong. So starting midway through my freshman year in college, I began a series of dating relationships that were my attempt to find love, acceptance and belonging.

During that next three years of college, I had to be dating at all times. If I didn't have someone to go out with, I knew that I would be un-happy, that I would have to face what I was feeling. I didn't want to do that. So I filled my time with relationships and with escape. I escaped into fantasy (go Trekkies!) and constant music. I escaped into the parties at my Sigma Chi fraternity house. And I was always starting a new relationship as soon as the old one ended. Sometimes in very awkward ways, the beginning of a new relationship overlapped with the ending of the old one.

Then, in the midst of my search for identity, belonging and love, I ran into Jim in the student union. He was working at a Christian book-table, engaging seeking people in spiritual conversations. I thought, *I eat Christians for lunch. I can ask a few devastating questions, and Jim will probably lose his faith.* So I gave him my best questions. How can a loving God send people to hell? How can an all-powerful God stand by and let so many innocent people suffer in the world? Why are some Christians so hypocritical? Why are they so narrow, uptight and judgmental toward other people? Why are they against premarital sex and homosexuality and people's freedom and fun?

Always before, well-meaning people had told me that I just had to have faith. Well I didn't have faith, so their answer never did me any good. But Jim didn't respond that way. He had thoughtful answers to my questions. He admitted when he didn't know something. He seemed to be taking me seriously. I felt listened to and cared for. And my heart began to open up.

As I watched Jim, he seemed to know who he was. He seemed to feel a sense of belonging wherever he went, and he gave other people that sense. He was at home with himself, and I felt more at home with myself when I was around him. So I began asking him questions. He told me he had found a life-changing relationship with God. Did I want that too?

I wasn't even sure what he was talking about. So he asked if I wanted to hear a brief summary of the message of the Christian faith. He asked if he could show me a picture of how I could find out who I was and where I belonged through a relationship with God.

"OK," I responded, though I was feeling awkward.

What Jim shared with me I now share with you. Over the years I've adapted it to make it clearer and more helpful. Hopefully this graphic summary of God's message to us, found in the Bible, will help you as much as it did me.

The Circle of Belonging

At first, all creation was in the circle of belonging.

God made the world. God made you—to love God, to be loved by God. We were made to have God at our center and through God to know we are God's children. With God in the center, we were in right relationship with ourselves and everything else.

Do you long to belong, to know who you are, to know you matter and are deeply and passionately loved by the God who made you? I know I wanted that. So what has happened? Why do we feel so alone, so distant from God?

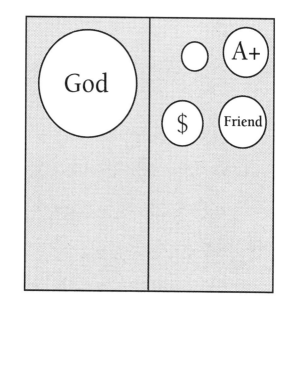

We loved other things more than God, resulting in spiritual death.

Unfortunately, we choose to substitute something else for God at the center of our lives. Maybe a boyfriend or girlfriend. Maybe a family or culture. Maybe achievement or performance. Maybe a role we play. Maybe our sexuality or gender, or approval from our parents or acceptance from our circle of friends. We forget that we are much more than any of these things.

Substituting something else for God at the center of our lives is what the Bible calls sin. And we all sin. We try to run our own lives, we try to create our own identity. We wrap our identity up in these other things, but they can't deliver and they will always disappoint us. Our lives become more fragmented, more painful, more scattered. At the center of our lives, where God

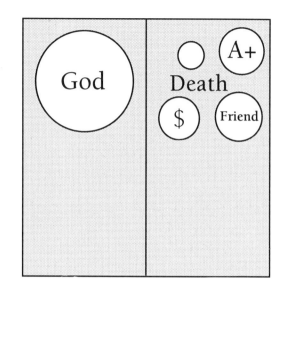

should be, we experience an emptiness.

I was seeking to wrap my life up in relationships and experiences. If I could only find the right girl, or experience the best high, I would feel better about life. I would discover who I really was. But it wasn't working. I still felt empty and often alone. How are you seeking to fill that emptiness and aloneness? Is it working for you?

In the Bible God tells us that as we reject God in favor of other things, we hurt ourselves, others and God. God hates our choice to replace God with other things. Without God in the center, our identity, our view of ourselves and our relationships with others are distorted. We often feel ashamed of who we are. We end up alone and disconnected. The lack of God at the center of our lives results in spiritual death. If we never turn toward God, that aloneness and emptiness

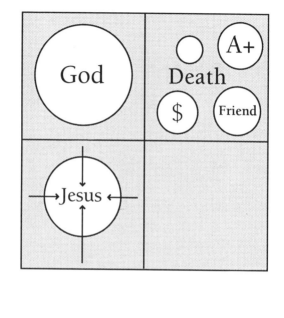

and spiritual death lasts forever! The Bible calls this condition hell.

To me this sounded harsh. Yet it made sense too. I knew I needed something more at the center of who I was. I was starting to want God back in the center. But how could that happen? What could I do?

Jesus died for us, taking on the death we deserve. Fortunately, God didn't leave us alone and spiritually dead. Out of passionate love for us, God wants to be restored as the center. God wants us to live in our identity as a loved child of God. So God came to us as a human being, Jesus.

Jesus was God. Jesus created love and acceptance and belonging wherever he went because God was his center. He showed people who they really were, and he showed people

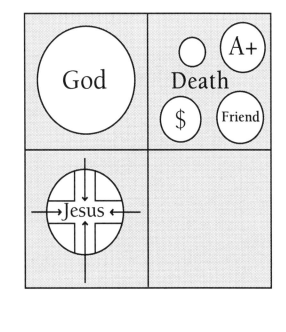

how to live with all those other things in right relationship with the real center.

And then, even though God was his center, he died for us. He was killed on the cross, taking on all the consequences of our choice to run our own lives and to live with other things at the center. At the cross Jesus took on himself the spiritual death we deserved.

Jesus offers us a way back into the circle of belonging.

What's more, Jesus didn't just die. He came back from death, and he is alive today. The evidence that Jesus rose from death is astonishing. He is alive! So he can live in us, at our center, restoring God to the central place in our lives. Jesus will forgive us for the pain we've caused and change us from the inside out. Jesus can give us the sense of belonging and identity we seek and

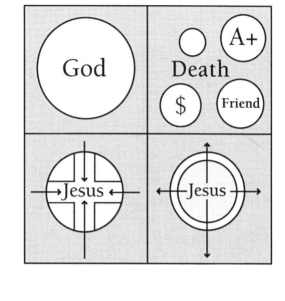

restore right relationships with others and the rest of creation. Because of Jesus we can live in our identity as God's child, part of God's family.

How does this happen?

☐ We *admit* our false centers and turn from them toward God.

☐ We *accept* Jesus' death for the death we deserve and the hurt we have caused.

☐ We *ask* Jesus to come into the center of our lives, and we *commit* ourselves to him as our forgiver, healer and leader. Through Jesus our real identity—God's beloved child—is reestablished in relationship with God.

Is God at the center of your life? Or is God somewhere else in your life, or even completely outside the circle of your life?

Asking Jesus into the center of your life is like

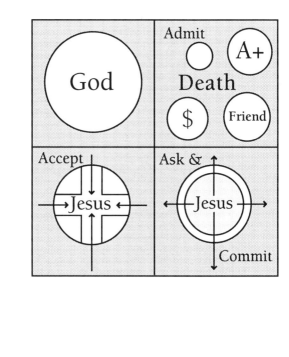

making a marriage commitment, like adoption into a new family. You don't understand all that you are committing yourself to when you start, but you know it will affect everything else in your life for the rest of your life!

There were aspects of my dating relationships, intense and often satisfying emotional and physical experiences, that I didn't want to give up. I knew Jesus would have something to say about those parts of my life. But I also knew that I wanted and needed something more at the center of my life. I needed a relationship with God.

Do you want that?

It has been years now since I committed my life to God, and I have never regretted it. God is at the center of my life. That gives me a sense of fulfillment and hope. And it has put all the other relationships in better perspective. I am no longer alone at the center of who I am. The God who made me has now made his home in me, and I have never been the same. I am now experiencing life as God's child, part of God's family.

You can pray a simple prayer to God as I did, and begin your new life with God at the center of who you are!

A Simple Prayer to Invite God into the Center of Your Life

Thank you, God, that you made me to know you and love you, to find love and belonging in a relationship with you at the center of my life, to be your beloved child.

I *admit* that I have replaced you at the center with other things and people, specifically *[in your own words, tell God what you have put before God in your life]*. I have hurt you and others, and

I choose now to turn from those things at the center of my life back to you, God.

I *accept* that Jesus on the cross took on himself my sin of putting other things before you, God, and that he took on my spiritual death. And I thank you that you loved me so much that you sent your Son to live and die for me.

I now *ask* you, Jesus, to come into the center of my life, and I *commit* myself to you as my forgiver, healer and leader. Thank you that you restore my relationship with God and others, and that you will now change me from the inside out! Thank you, Jesus!

Helping You Get Started

If you have made this commitment and asked Jesus to come into the center of your life, you're now beginning the greatest adventure

27

there is: growing your life with God. God will change you from the inside out. God will give you strength and wisdom to have new priorities and to relate to people in new ways. God is with you all the way and actually lives inside you by the gift of the Holy Spirit. Rejoice that you now live in the reality of being a beloved child of God!

How do you grow your life with God? Again, picture life with Jesus at the center. The arrows point to the key ways you can grow your life with God.

The upward arrow points toward your direct, conversational relationship with God. You can nurture that by spending time each day reading the Bible and then talking to God. When you read the Bible, you can start with a Gospel account of Jesus, say, the Gospel of John. When you talk to God, use simple lan-

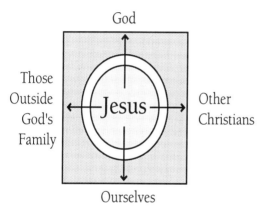

God

Those
Outside
God's
Family

Jesus

Other
Christians

Ourselves

guage. Speak praise for God's beauty, tenderness and power, give thanks for what God has done, and then bring your life before God and make your requests for the day. Make sure to spend a few moments quietly listening for any direction or encouragement God may want to give you. As you listen, you will sometimes have a sense in your heart of something God wants to say to you about your life or about the Scripture you have just read. Start praying and listening to God and reading the Bible for at least fifteen minutes a day.

Back to the drawing: One sideways arrow represents your relationships with other Christians. Your life with God won't grow unless you spend time with others in God's family, being encouraged, getting wisdom, asking for their prayers and just hanging out.

The other sideways arrow points toward others who are not yet in God's family. They need Jesus at the center of their lives too, and we get the privilege of telling them what God has done for us. Begin by sharing with a friend who doesn't know Jesus a few simple words on what God has just done in your life.

The downward arrow represents your relationship with yourself, your sexuality, your culture and your place in your family. God will begin to heal and restore you in these parts of your life. You can now trust God for new attitudes, new confidence to become who he made you to be.

God loves you. You were made for belonging and identity with God at the center of your life. God is with you and lives inside you by the Holy Spirit. Grow your life with God! It is the most extraordinary and transforming adventure there is.

If you've made this commitment, please let me know at <Rick_Richardson@ivstaff.org>. To be honest, your courageous choice will encourage me a lot! And I'd like to pray for you as you begin this great adventure.

Rick Richardson (M.Div., Northern Baptist Seminary) is national field director for evangelism for InterVarsity Christian Fellowship/USA. Previously he served as pastor of evangelism for Church of the Resurrection (Wheaton, Illinois). He is also the author of Evangelism Outside the Box *(InterVarsity Press).*